Fr. Paul Trinchard, S.T.L.

MY

BASIC

MISSAL

Published by

MAETA
METAIRIE LOUISIANA

i

Published by MAETA

Printed in the United States of America

Library of Congress Catalog Number: 96-76329

ISBN 1-889168-00-9

Editor's Note:

In 1996, Rev. Dr. Malachi Martin reviewed Fr. Trinchard's exegesis of the Canonized Latin Mass Prayers for the Ordinary of the Mass. The following are his remarks:

"As more and more of the Catholic laity return to attendance at the immemorial Latin Mass, there is a felt need for a vernacular translation which is accurate and reverential. Fr. Trinchard's exegesis of the Missal meets this need. No greater praise can be given of this work than to say that Pope St. Gregory the Great who codified our beautiful Mass in the 6th century, would have been wholly enthusiastic for this translation–its grace, accuracy, prayerfulness. I have shown it to several officials in the Roman congregation. They singly praise it highly."

† *Malachi Martin* (R.I.P.)

MY BASIC MISSAL

FOREWORD

In spite of being properly ordained, from 1966 until 1992, I was forced by bishops to co-celebrate with the people, the Mass-like Novus Ordo Services. I broke ranks and began saying the Canonized Latin Mass in 1992.

Often at night, I would awaken with Canonized Mass prayers going through my mind. During these times, I studied and prayed the Canonized Latin Mass prayers.

MY BASIC MISSAL is the fruit of God's night-school on my behalf. In this, my missal, I give you my translations/exegesis of the fixed priest-prayers of the Canonized Mass Liturgy of the Latin Rite.

The Priest has to say all the prayers of the Mass. The advantage of the laity, as it were, is that each can pray the Mass as God inspires. Therefore, don't feel constrained to *keep up with the Priest.* Don't worry about praying all the prayers. Pray as few or as many prayers as you desire. The main goal is to pray the Mass as best you can.

Fr. Paul Trinchard

MEDITATION BEFORE MASS

You and I are wretched *sinners*--sinners by birth and inclination; and sinners in deed and habit. *Sin* is the very worst present evil. Why? Only *sin* brings one to eternal Hell. Only *sin* damns eternally.

You and I are naturally-born wretched *sinners*. As such, we *deserve* awesome eternal sufferings. At the very least, we do *not* deserve Heaven. Since eternity is infinitely longer than present life, your eternal need is of infinite importance to you. *If* you see this and are sane, your *only* need is *THE* Saviour. That's your greatest need. That's your only real need (Mk 8:36).

Even though we are cursed into darkness, light is given so as to enable each to seek and initially receive, by God's free gift of grace (Eph 2:8) *THE* Saviour. Those who keep the grace are the *quotquot* of John's first chapter. They accept Christ as *THE* Saviour. *Quotquot* are given the *power* or potential to become eternal "sons of God (Jn 1:12)."

God's greatest gift, the Canonized Mass, fulfills your greatest and only real need. Divine Liturgy is *THE* Saving Deed among us, accomplished by God's infinite power and given because of God's infinite love. The Saving Deed is so awesome that it results in the Saving Person coming to us.

Pray the Canonized Mass Liturgy so as, by God's grace and your own graced cooperation, you may come to live, not you, but Christ in you–Christ, Holy Sacrifice and Holy Eucharist.

Several modern popes give us the proper direction for lay participation in the Mass. For example, Pope Pius XII stated:

> **"To participate in the Eucharistic Sacrifice is the chief duty and supreme dignity of the faithful.**
>
> **They should strive to be united as closely as possible with the High Priest...**
>
> **Together with Him and through Him, let them make their oblation;**
>
> **And in union with Him, let them offer up themselves."**
> *Mediator Dei,* Pope Pius XII, 1947

✠

ORDO MISSAE

THE ORDINARY OF THE MASS
(Unchangeable Parts of the Mass)

I. MASS OF THE CATECHUMENS

BEGINNING OF MASS

IN NOMINE PATRIS, et Filii,✠ et Spiritus Sancti. Amen.
IN the NAME of the FATHER, and of the Son, ✠ and of the Holy Ghost. Amen.

P. Introibo ad altare Dei.
I will go unto the altar of God.
S. Ad Deum qui laetificat juventutem meam.
To God, who giveth joy to my youth.

The Priest prays his Mass intention:

I, the Christ-priest, will go unto God's altar to bring into our here and now, Christ's Holy Sacrifice, *the* Saving Action, the *only* means of salvation from Hell unto Heaven.

Pray the following psalm while the Priest and Server pray the dialogue:

O GOD, champion my cause against faithless people. Rescue me from evil and deceitful men. Indeed, Thou art my God, my only strength, my only hope. Why does loneliness envelope me? Why does the enemy's oppression sadden me? Comfort me, O God, with Thy truth. Lead me into Thy light. Bring me unto Thy holy mountain--Thy Sacrifice and Thy abiding Presence.

Here is Thy Sanctuary; here is Thine altar. Here art Thou, my God, my life and my joy. I adore Thee, O God, my God.

Glory be to the Father, and to the Son and to the Holy Ghost, as it was in the beginning, is now and ever shall be, world without end. Amen.

JUDICA ME--PSALM 42

P. *Judica me, Deus, et discerne causam meam de gente non sancta: ab homine iniquo et doloso erue me.*
Give judgment for me, O God, and decide my cause against an unholy people: from unjust and deceitful men deliver me.

S. *Quia tu es Deus fortitudo mea: quare me repulisti, et quare tristis incedo, dum affligit me inimicus?*
For Thou, O God, art my strength: why hast Thou forsaken me? And why do I go about in sadness, while the enemy afflicts me?

P. *Emitte lucem tuam et veritatem tuam: ipsa me deduxerunt et adduxerunt in montem sanctum tuum, et in tabernacula tua.*
Send forth Thy light and Thy truth: for they have led me and brought me to Thy holy hill and Thy dwelling place.

S. *Et introibo ad altare Dei: ad Deum qui laetificat juventutem meam.*
And I will go in to the altar of God, to God, the joy of my youth.

P. Confitebor tibi in cithara, Deus, Deus meus: quare tristis es anima mea, et quare conturbas me?
I shall yet praise Thee upon the harp, O God, my God. Why art thou sad, my soul, and why dost thou trouble me?

S. Spera in Deo, quoniam adhuc confitebor illi: salutare vultus mei, et Deus meus.
Trust in God, for I shall yet praise Him, the salvation of my countenance, and my God.

P. Gloria Patri, et Filio, et Spiritui Sancto.
Glory be to the Father, and to the Son, and to the Holy Ghost.
S. Sicut erat in principio, et nunc, et semper: et in saecula saeculorum. Amen.
As it was in the beginning, is now, and ever shall be, world without end. Amen.

P. Introibo ad altare Dei.
I will go in to the altar of God.
S. Ad Deum qui laetificat juventutem meam.
To God, the joy of my youth.

P. Adjutorium nostrum ✠ *in nomine Domini.*
Our help ✠ **is in the name of the Lord.**

S. Qui fecit coelum et terram.
Who hath made heaven and earth.

4

CONFITEOR

P. Confiteor Deo omnipotenti, etc. (as below)

S. Misereatur tui omnipotens Deus, et dimissis peccatis tuis, perducat te ad vitam aeternam.
May the Almighty God have mercy upon thee, forgive thee thy sins and bring thee to life everlasting.
P. Amen.

CONFITEOR Deo omnipotenti, beatae Mariae semper Virgini, beato Michaeli Archangelo, beato Joanni Baptistae, sanctis Apostolis Petro et Paulo, omnibus Sanctis, et tibi, Pater: quia peccavi nimis cogitatione, verbo et opere: **(strike the breast three times)** *mea culpa, mea culpa, mea maxima culpa. Ideo precor beatam Mariam semper Virginem, beatum Michaelem Archangelum, beatum Joannem Baptistam, sanctos Apostolos Petrum et Paulum, omnes Sanctos, et te, Pater, orare pro me ad Dominum Deum nostrum.*

I CONFESS to Almighty God, to Blessed Mary ever Virgin, to Blessed Michael the Archangel, to Blessed John the Baptist, to the Holy Apostles Peter and Paul, and to all the Saints, and to you, Father, that I have sinned exceedingly in thought, word and deed, *(strike the breast three times)* **through my fault, through my fault, through my most grievous fault. Therefore, I beseech Blessed Mary, ever Virgin, Blessed Michael**

5

the Archangel, Blessed John the Baptist, the Holy Apostles Peter and Paul, and all the Saints, and you Father, to pray to the Lord our God for me.

P. Misereatur vestri omnipotens Deus, et dimissis peccatis vestris, perducat vos ad vitam aeternam.
May the Almighty God have mercy on you, forgive you your sins, and bring you to life everlasting.
S. Amen.

P. Indulgentiam, ✠ absolutionem, et remissionem peccatorum nostrorum tribuat nobis omnipotens et misericors Dominus.
May the Almighty and Merciful Lord grant us pardon, ✠ absolution, and remission of our sins.
S. Amen.

~~~~~~

Pray with the priest as he prays for himself and for us:

 May Almighty God grant us salvation from Hell unto Heaven. May God forgive us our sins.

O GOD, as Thou freely bestoweth Salvation, only thus is Salvation granted. Grant us Salvation, for only then will Salvation be given. Hear our one and only prayer, O Lord. We pray for Salvation.

~~~~~~

P. Deus, tu conversus vivificabis nos.
Thou wilt turn, O God, and bring us to life.
S. Et plebs tua laetabitur in te.
And Thy people shall rejoice in Thee.
P. Ostende nobis, Domine, misericordiam tuam.
Show us, O Lord, Thy mercy.
S. Et salutare tuum da nobis.
And grant us Thy salvation.

P. Domine, exaudi orationem meam.
O Lord, hear my prayer.
S. Et clamor meus ad te veniat.
And let my cry come unto Thee.
P. Dominus vobiscum. **The Lord be with you.**
S. Et cum spiritu tuo. **And with thy spirit.**
P. Oremus. **Let us pray.**

INTROIBO AD ALTARE DEI

AUFER a nobis, quaesumus, Domine, iniquitates nostras: ut ad Sancta sanctorum puris mereamur mentibus introire. Per Christum Dominum nostrum. Amen.
TAKE AWAY from us our iniquities, O LORD, that being made pure in heart, we may be made worthy to enter into the Holy of Holies. Through Christ our Lord. Amen.

7

ORAMUS te, Domine, per merita Sanctorum tuorum, quorum reliquiae hic sunt, et omnium Sanctorum: ut indulgere digneris omnia peccata mea. Amen.

WE BESEECH THEE, O LORD, that through the merits of Thy saints whose relics I kiss and of all the other saints, grant me forgiveness of all my sins. Amen.

 The ordained Priest goes to the Altar *in persona Christi* to offer the Sacrifice of Christ--your only Need, God's Greatest Gift. Christ-priest now enters the Holy of Holies – *ut ad Sancta Sanctorum* – in order to offer *the* Sacrifice for our sins – God's Divine Liturgy.

O LORD, grant me the grace to adequately respond to SO GREAT SALVATION – the Holy Sacrifice of the Mass!

*● INTROIT--*PROPER--Today's Mass ●

KYRIE ELEISON

P. Kyrie eleison.	**Lord, have mercy on us.**
S. *Kyrie eleison.*	**Lord, have mercy on us.**
P. Kyrie eleison.	**Lord, have mercy on us.**
S. *Christe eleison.*	**Christ, have mercy on us.**
P. Christe eleison.	**Christ, have mercy on us.**
S. *Christe eleison.*	**Christ, have mercy on us.**
P. Kyrie eleison.	**Lord, have mercy on us.**
S. *Kyrie eleison.*	**Lord, have mercy on us.**
P. Kyrie eleison.	**Lord, have mercy on us.**

GLORIA

"Glory to God..." At this point in the Divine Liturgy, we speak well of God—we *bene-dicimus Te.* Later, at the Consecration, when Christ-priest, in the name of God *blesses,* God's great salutary metamorphosis is realized (in a mystical/sacramental way).

GLORIA in excelsis Deo, et in terra pax hominibus bonae voluntatis. Laudamus te. Benedicimus te. Adoramus te. Glorificamus te. Gratias agimus tibi propter magnam gloriam tuam. Domine Deus, Rex coelestis. Deus Pater omnipotens. Domine Fili unigenite,

9

Jesu Christe. Domine Deus, Agnus Dei, Filius Patris. Qui tollis peccata mundi, miserere nobis. Qui tollis peccata mundi, suscipe deprecationem nostram. Qui sedes ad dexteram Patris, miserere nobis. Quoniam tu solus Sanctus. Tu solus Dominus. Tu solus Altissimus, Jesu Christe. Cum Sancto Spiritu, ✠ in gloria Dei Patris. Amen.

GLORY to God in the highest. And on earth peace to men of good will. We praise Thee. We bless Thee--*we speak well of Thee.* We adore Thee. We glorify Thee. We give Thee thanks for Thy great glory. O Lord God, heavenly King, God the Father Almighty, O Lord Jesus Christ, the Only-begotten Son, O Lord God, Lamb of God, Son of the Father: Who takest away the sins of the world, have mercy on us, Who sittest at the right hand of the Father, have mercy on us, for Thou alone art holy, Thou alone are the Lord, Thou alone, O Jesus Christ, are most high, together with the Holy Ghost ✠ in the glory of God the Father. Amen.

P. Dominus vobiscum. **The Lord be with you.**
S. Et cum spiritu tuo. **And with thy spirit.**
P. OREMUS. **Let us pray.**

● *ORATIO* (PRAYER)--PROPER--Today's Mass ●

The Priest reads the **EPISTLE** or LESSON from the **PROPER** of today's Mass, and the **Gradual** and **Tract**. At the end of the EPISTLE:

S. Deo gratias. **Thanks be to God.**
The Priest prays:

MUNDA cor meum, ac labia mea, omnipotens Deus, qui labia Isaiae prophetae calculo mundasti ignito: ita me tua grata miseratione dignare mundare, ut sanctum Evangelium tuum digne valeam nuntiare. Per Christum Dominum nostrum. Amen.

CLEANSE my heart and my lips, O Almighty God, Who cleansed the lips of the prophet Isaias with a burning coal. In Thy gracious mercy deign so to purify me that I may worthily proclaim Thy Holy Gospel, through Christ our Lord. Amen.

Jube Domine benedicere.
Vouchsafe, O Lord, to bless me.

Dominus sit in corde meo, et in labiis meis; ut digne et competenter annuntiem Evangelium suum. Amen.
May the Lord be in my heart and on my lips that I may worthily and fittingly proclaim His Gospel. Amen.

11

P. Dominus vobiscum. **The Lord be with you.**

S. Et cum spiritu tuo. **And with thy spirit.**

P. ✠ Sequentia (vel Initium) sancti Evangelii secundum N...

✠ **The continuation (or the beginning) of the Holy Gospel according to Saint N...**

S. Gloria tibi, Domine. **Glory be to Thee, O Lord.**

The Priest makes the Sign of the Cross on the book and on forehead, lips and breast.

Stand as the Priest reads the **GOSPEL** for today's Mass.

● *GOSPEL*--PROPER--Today's Mass ●

S. Laus tibi, Christe.
Praise be to Thee, O Christ.

Kissing the book, the Priest says:

P. Per evangelica dicta deleantur nostra delicta.
By the words of the Gospel, may our sins be taken away.

After the **GOSPEL**, the Priest gives a sermon. The sermon is part of the liturgy of the Priest's Mass. By giving the sermon, the Priest acts as Christ to his flock.

NICENE CREED

CREDO in unum Deum, Patrem omnipotentem, factorem coeli et terrae, visibilium omnium et invisibilium. Et in unum Dominum Jesum Christum, Filium Dei unigenitum. Et ex Patre natum, ante omnia saecula. Deum de Deo, lumen de lumine, Deum verum de Deo vero. Genitum, non factum, consubstantialem Patri: per quem omnia facta sunt. Qui propter nos homines et propter nostram salutem descendit de coelis. (Genuflect):

ET INCARNATUS EST DE SPIRITU SANCTO EX MARIA VIRGINE: ET HOMO FACTUS EST. (Rise)

Crucifixus etiam pro nobis; sub Pontio Pilato passus, et sepultus est. Et resurrexit tertia die, secundum Scripturas. Et ascendit in coelum: sedet ad dexteram Patris. Et iterum venturus est cum gloria judicare vivos et mortuos: cujus regni non erit finis.

Et in Spiritum Sanctum, Dominum et vivificantem: qui ex Patre, Filioque procedit. Qui cum Patre, et Filio simul adoratur, et conglorificatur: qui locutus est per prophetas. Et unam, sanctam, Catholicam et Apostolicam Ecclesiam. Confiteor unum baptisma in remissionem peccatorum. Et exspecto resurrectionem mortuorum. ✠ *Et vitam venturi saeculi. Amen.*

14

I BELIEVE in one God, the Father Almighty, Creator of heaven and earth, and in all things visible and invisible. And in one Lord Jesus Christ, the Only-begotten Son of God. Born of the Father before all ages. God of God; Light of Light; true God of true God. Begotten not made; of one being with the Father; by Whom all things were made. Who for us men, and for our salvation, came down from heaven. (Genuflect.)

AND WAS MADE FLESH BY THE HOLY GHOST OF THE VIRGIN MARY: AND WAS MADE MAN. (Rise.)

He was also crucified for us, suffered under Pontius Pilate and was buried. And on the third day He rose again according to the Scriptures. And ascending into heaven, He sits at the right hand of the Father. And He shall come again in glory to judge the living and the dead; and of His kingdom there shall be no end.

And I believe in the Holy Ghost, the Lord and Giver of Life, Who proceeds from the Father and the Son, Who together with the Father and the Son is adored and glorified: Who spoke by the prophets. And I believe in One, Holy, Catholic and Apostolic Church. I confess one baptism for the remission of sins. And I await the resurrection of the dead ✠ and the life of the world to come. Amen.

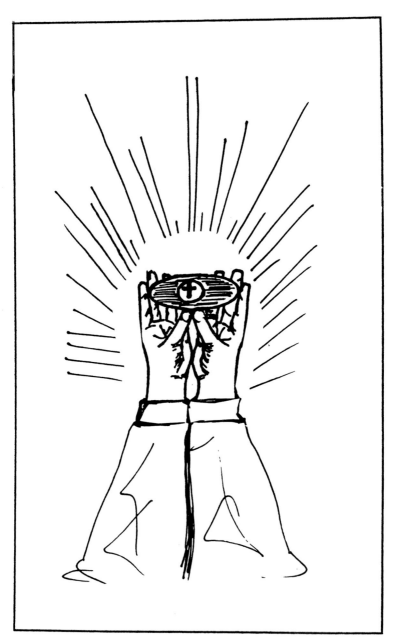

II. MASS OF THE FAITHFUL

THE OFFERTORY

P. *Dominus vobiscum.* **The Lord be with you.**
S. *Et cum spiritu tuo.* **And with thy spirit.**
P. *Oremus.* **Let us pray.** (Sit.)

●*OFFERTORY*--PROPER--Today's Mass ●

~~~~~~

At each valid Mass, the Priest *in persona Christi, as Christ,* offers Christ. The Offerer and the Offered renews His *Effective* Saving Will. Through His anointed Priest, Christ renews or re-does His Will with such awesome God-power that the Sacrifice of Calvary and Christ Himself *truly and sacramentally come into being.* Christ *was from His beginning, is now* and *will always be* both *the Priest* and *the Immaculate Victim.*

~~~~~~

Lifting the host on the paten, the Priest prays:

17

SUSCIPE, sancte Pater, omnipotens aeterne Deus, hanc immaculatam Hostiam, quam ego indignus famulus tuus offero tibi, Deo meo vivo et vero, pro innumerabilibus peccatis, et offensionibus, et negligentiis meis, et pro omnibus circumstantibus, sed et pro omnibus fidelibus Christianis vivis atque defunctis: ut mihi et illis proficiat ad salutem in vitam aeternam. Amen.

ACCEPT, O Holy Father, Almighty and Eternal God, THE Immaculate Victim Whom I, Thy unworthy servant, offer unto Thee, to atone for my numberless sins, offenses, and negligences; on behalf of all here present and likewise for all faithful Catholics, living and dead, that it may profit me and them unto joy in Heaven. Amen.

~~~~~~

The Priest, in persona Christi, offers Christ, *not* bread or wine. Christ, sacrificed for our sins, is our *only* hope of salvation from Hell unto Heaven. Therefore, the IMMACULATE VICTIM--*HANC IMMACULATAM HOSTIAM*--is offered.

After Pentecost, only Catholics have potential to be saved–as dogmatically defined by the Church in times past. Up to 1950 or so, *Christian* was synonymous with *Catholic*. The Elect, at least at the moment of their death, are Catholics – in spirit and in truth.

~~~~~~

DEUS QUI

While he mixes the drop of water with the wine, the Priest prays as follows:

DEUS ✠ *qui humanae substantiae dignitatem mirabiliter condidisti, et mirabilius reformasti: da nobis per hujus aquae et vini mysterium, ejus divinitatis esse consortes, qui humanitatis nostrae fieri dignatus est particeps, Jesus Christus Filius tuus Dominus noster: Qui tecum vivit et regnat in unitate Spiritus Sancti Deus: per omnia saecula saeculorum. Amen.*

O GOD ✠ Who established the nature of man in wondrous dignity, and still more admirably restored it, grant that through the mystery of this water and wine, we may be made partakers of His Divinity, *(consortes)* Who deigned to partake of our humanity *(particeps)* Jesus Christ, Thy Son, our Lord: Who with Thee lives and reigns in the unity of the Holy Ghost, God, world without end. Amen.

OFFERIMUS

~~~~~~

Through and with Thy Christ-priest, I offer *Christ.* I offer myself to Christ.

I invite Christ to live in me, to suffer and to die. Thus do I participate in Mass. Thus do I live the Mass. *Offero, tibi, Domine, calicem salutaris!*

~~~~~~

The Priest returns to the center to offer *calicem salutaris:*

OFFERIMUS tibi, Domine, calicem salutaris tuam deprecantes clementiam: ut in conspectu divinae majestatis tuae, pro nostra et totius mundi salute cum odore suavitatis ascendat. Amen.

WE OFFER to Thee, O Lord, THE CHALICE OF SALVATION seeking Thy loving mercy that it may benefit us and others unto salvation from Hell. Amen.

IN SPIRITU HUMILITATIS

Making the Sign of the Cross with the chalice and placing it on the corporal, he covers it with the pall:

IN SPIRITU HUMILITATIS, et in animo contrito suscipiamur a te, Domine: et sic fiat sacrificium nostrum in conspectu tuo hodie, ut placeat tibi, Domine Deus.

IN A HUMBLE SPIRIT and with a contrite heart may we be accepted by Thee, O Lord, and may our sacrifice so be offered in Thy sight this day so as to please Thee, O Lord God.

~~~~~~

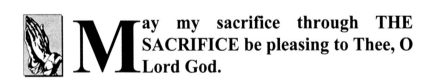**M**ay my sacrifice through THE SACRIFICE be pleasing to Thee, O Lord God.

~~~~~~

VENI SANCTIFICATOR

Deign, O Lord, to BLESS (divinely transform) through Thy validly functioning Christ-priest. BLESS through THE Saving-Person and His Saving-Deed. BLESS through Christ living in me unto my dying in Him. Bring about my eternal oblation through and in Thy Saving-Deed, soon to be made present again in our here and now in a mystical/sacramental manner.

Raising his eyes and blessing the offering, the Priest prays:

VENI, Sanctificator omnipotens aeterne Deus: et bene ✠ dic hoc sacrificium, tuo sancto nomini praeparatum.

COME, Holy Ghost, Almighty Eternal God and bless ✠ this Sacrifice prepared in Thy name.

LAVABO--PSALM 25:6-12

The Priest washes his fingers and recites these verses from Psalm 25:

LAVABO inter innocentes manus meas: et circumdabo altare tuum, Domine. Ut audiam vocem laudis: et enarrem universa mirabilia tua. Domine, dilexi decorem domus tuae: et locum habitationis gloriae tuae.

I will wash my hands in innocence, and will go around Thy altar, O Lord. That I may hear the voice of praise, and tell of all Thy wondrous deeds. O Lord, I love the beauty of Thy house and the place where Thy glory dwelleth.

Ne perdas cum impiis, Deus animam meam: et cum viris sanguinum vitam meam. In quorum manibus iniquitates sunt: dextera eorum repleta est muneribus. Ego autem in innocentia mea ingressus sum: redime me, et miserere mei. Pes meus stetit in directo: in ecclesiis benedicam te, Domine.

Gather not my soul with the wicked: nor my life with men of blood. In whose hands are iniquities and their right hand is filled with bribes. But as for me, I walk in innocence, redeem me and have mercy on me. My foot is on the straight way; in the churches I will bless Thee, O Lord.

Gloria Patri, et Filio, et Spiritui Sancto. Sicut erat in principio, et nunc, et semper, et in saecula saeculorum. Amen.

Glory be to the Father and to the Son and to the Holy Ghost, as it was in the beginning, is now and ever shall be, world without end. Amen.

Prepare to offer yourself in sacrifice with Christ as the Saving-Deed comes to us through the action of the Christ-priest:

OLord, I submit myself to Thee, through, with and in Thy Saving Deed!

SUSCIPE

Bowing, with hands joined, the Priest says:

SUSCIPE, sancta Trinitas, hanc oblationem, quam tibi offerimus ob memoriam passionis, resurrectionis et ascensionis Jesu Christi Domini nostri: et in honorem beatae Mariae semper Virginis, et beati Joannis Baptistae, et sanctorum Apostolorum Petri et Pauli, et istorum, et omnium Sanctorum: ut illis proficiat ad honorem, nobis autem ad salutem: et illi pro nobis intercedere dignentur in coelis, quorum memoriam agimus in terris. Per eumdem Christum Dominum nostrum. Amen.

ACCEPT, most Holy Trinity, *hanc oblationem* (by Christ-priest at this *his* Mass, and by each through, in and unto Christ's Oblation) *ob memoriam* (which flows out of and is the Memory: Christ's Passion, Resurrection, and Ascension) in honor of Blessed Mary, ever Virgin, Blessed John the Baptist, the Holy Apostles Peter and Paul, and all other saints that it may avail to their honor and aid our salvation; we beg the saints in Heaven to intercede for us who honor their memory here on earth. Amen.

M ost Holy Trinity, accept my life-oblation through THE Christ-oblation and into the Memory of the Passion, Resurrection and Ascension of Jesus Christ. Save me from the Hell I deserve through Jesus Christ, Our Lord and Saviour.

ORATE FRATRES

Kissing the altar, turning to the people, the Priest prays:

ORATE, FRATRES, ut meum ac vestrum sacrificium acceptabile fiat apud Deum Patrem omnipotentem.
PRAY, BRETHREN, that my sacrifice and yours *(hanc oblationem)* **may be acceptable before God, the Father Almighty.**

S. Suscipiat Dominus sacrificium de manibus tuis ad laudem et gloriam nominis sui, ad utilitatem quoque nostram, totiusque Ecclesiae suae sanctae.
May the Lord receive *the* **sacrifice (this your Mass) at thy hands to the praise and glory of His name, for our benefit and that of all His holy Church. Amen.**

~~~~~~

Lord, receive at the hands of Thy Christ-priest, this Holy Sacrifice of Mass, the *only Sacrifice* **which renders holy or acceptable to Thee, any and all life-oblations or sacrifices.**

~~~~~~

P. Per omnia saecula saeculorum.
World without end.
S. Amen.

PREFACE--CANON

P. Dominus vobiscum. **The Lord be with you.**
S. Et cum spiritu tuo. **And with thy spirit.**
P. Sursum corda. **Lift up your hearts.**

S. Habemus ad Dominum.
We have them lifted up to the Lord.

P. Gratias agamus Domino Deo nostro.
Let us give thanks to the Lord our God.

S. Dignum et justum est.
It is fitting and just.

The Priest now says the solemn, yet variable, prayer which introduces or "prefaces" the Canon prayer. The following preface is often used on Sundays:

Vere dignum et justum est, aequum et salutare, nos tibi semper, et ubique gratias agere: Domine sancte, Pater omnipotens, aeterne Deus: Qui cum unigenito Filio tuo, et Spiritu Sancto, unus es Deus, unus es Dominus: non in unius singularitate personae, sed in unius Trinitate substantiae. Quod enim de tua gloria, revelante te, credimus, hoc de Filio tuo, hoc de Spiritu Sancto, sine differentia discretionis sentimus. Ut in confessione verae sempiternaeque Deitatis, et in personis proprietas, et in essentia unitas, et in majestate adoretur aequalitas. Quam laudant Angeli atque Archangeli, Cherubim quoque ac Seraphim: qui non cessant clamare quotidie, una voce dicentes: Here the bell is rung three times.

SANCTUS, SANCTUS, SANCTUS! Dominus Deus Sabaoth, Pleni sunt coeli, et terra gloria tua. Hosanna in excelsis. Benedictus qui venit in nomine Domini. Hosanna in excelsis!

It is truly meet and just, right and profitable for our salvation, for, at all times and in all places, to give thanks unto Thee, O holy Lord, Father Almighty, Everlasting God; Who, together with Thine Only-begotten Son, and the Holy Ghost, art one God, one Lord; not in the oneness of a single Person, but in the Trinity of one substance. For that which we believe by the revelation of Thy glory, the same do we believe of Thy Son, the same of the Holy Ghost, without difference or inequality. We confess the True and

Everlasting Godhead, distinct in Persons and united in Essence. We adore Thee as we join the angels, archangels, cherubim and seraphim who with one voice continually praise and adore Thee as they say:

HOLY, HOLY, HOLY! Lord God Almighty! Heaven and earth are full of Thy Glory. Hosanna in the highest! Blessed is He Who cometh in the Name of the Lord. Hosanna in the highest!

HOSANNA! Save us! Thy Saving-Deed is about to materialize in our midst. Out of *Thy Holy Sacrifice* will come *Thy Holy Sacrament.*

Father, as Thou created, now Thou blesseth. Bless into being the Eternal Oblation, Heaven: the soon to be present Lamb Once Slain and those of us, the Elect, who have been or will be, oblated: through, with and in the Lamb, Jesus Christ. God our Father, please BLESS me into being oblated through, with and in Christ.

TE IGITUR
(FIRST PRAYER OF THE CANON)

TE IGITUR, clementissime Pater, per Jesum Christum Filium tuum, Dominum nostrum, supplices rogamus, ac petimus, (He kisses the Altar) *uti accepta habeas, et benedicas haec* ✠ *dona, haec* ✠ *munera, haec* ✠ *sancta sacrificia illibata; in primis, quae tibi offerimus pro Ecclesia tua sancta catholica: quam pacificare, custodire, adunare, et regere digneris toto orbe terrarum: una cum famulo tuo Papa nostro N... et Antistite nostro N... et omnibus orthodoxis, atque catholicae et apostolicae fidei cultoribus.*

Therefore, because of He Who comes in Thy name, we whose only need is salvation, ask and beseech Thee, most kind heavenly Father, through Thy Son our Lord, that Thou wilt accept and *bless* **into being** *His Oblation:* **that which Thou hast given to us** ✠ *(haec dona);* **that which we have developed** ✠ *(haec munera)*; **these material things** *BREAD AND WINE* **to be metamorphasized into** *THE* **Holy Sacrifice** ✠ *(haec sancta sacrificia illibata).*

First of all, we offer *THE* **Sacrifice for Thy holy and Catholic Church. Deign to rule** *(regere),* **unite** *(adunare),* **preserve** *(custodire)* **and perfect in Thy**

peace *(pacificare)* Thy whole existential Church throughout the world, especially N..., our Pope, and N..., our bishop. May all of these be brought *into,* or preserved in the one family of true believers, those who embrace and practice the apostolic and Catholic faith unto salvation.

MEMENTO

MEMENTO, Domine, famulorum famularumque tuarum N... et N..., et omnium circumstantium, quorum tibi fides cognita est, et nota devotio, pro quibus tibi offerimus: vel qui tibi offerunt hoc sacrificium laudis pro se, suisque omnibus: pro redemptione animarum suarum, pro spe salutis et incolumitatis suae: tibique reddunt vota sua aeterno Deo, vivo et vero.

MEMENTO, O Lord, the members of Thy family, Thy servants and handmaids N... and N... and all here present, whose faith and devotion are known to Thee, for whom we offer, or who offer up to Thee, this Sacrifice of praise for themselves and all those dear to them, for the redemption of their souls, for the true virtue of hope *(pro spe salutis)*; and for the removal of obstacles to salvation *(incolumitatis suae)*. To Thee, Eternal Living and True God, they render their total dedication.

Memento, *Domine*...make us and those for whom we pray, we beseech Thee, O Lord, partakers of *the* Memory.

Memento, Domine...that's *all* we pray for. Make me now a partaker of Thy Memory.

Make me part of Christ-suffering and Christ-dying. Only thus will I be part of *the Eternal Memory*, the glorified Christ.

COMMUNICANTES

COMMUNICANTES, et memoriam venerantes, in primis gloriosae semper Virginis Mariae, Genitricis Dei et Domini nostri Jesu Christi: sed et beatorum Apostolorum ac Martyrum tuorum, Petri et Pauli, Andreae, Jacobi, Joannis, Thomae, Jacobi, Philippi, Bartholomaei, Matthaei, Simonis et Thaddaei: Lini, Cleti, Clementis, Xysti, Cornelii, Cypriani, Laurentii, Chrysogoni, Joannis et Pauli, Cosmae et Damiani: et omnium Sanctorum tuorum; quorum meritis precibusque concedas, ut in omnibus protectionis tuae muniamur auxilio. Per eumdem Christum Dominum nostrum. Amen.

VENERATING the memories (lives) of the saints and desiring to be united with them--the glorious ever Virgin Mary, Mother of our God and Lord, Jesus Christ; the blessed Apostles and Martyrs, Peter and Paul, Andrew, James, John, Thomas, James, Philip, Bartholomew, Matthew, Simon and Thaddeus, Linus, Cletus, Clement, Sixtus, Cornelius, Cyprian, Lawrence, Chrysogonus, John and Paul, Cosmas and Damien, and all Thy saints--grant O, Lord, for the sake of their merits and prayers that in all things we may be guarded and helped by their intercessions on our behalf. Through the same Jesus Christ our Lord. Amen.

HANC IGITUR

~~~~~~

For over a millenium, God's Jewish priests placed their hands over sacrificial victims. Now the Christ-priest does this to you, *if* you are willing to be so sacrificed. This prayer plus the *QUAM OBLATIONEM* emphasize *your* oblation into the Christ-oblation.

~~~~~~

HANC IGITUR oblationem servitutis nostrae, sed et cunctae familiae tuae, quaesumus, Domine, ut placatus accipias: diesque nostros in tua pace disponas, atque ab aeterna damnatione nos eripi, et in electorum tuorum jubeas grege numerari. Per Christum Dominum nostrum. Amen.

Do Thou, O Lord, be pleased to bring about the desired oblation of our lives in and into *the* Oblation. Grant us Thy divine peace in this life. Grant us salvation from eternal damnation. Number us among the Elect in Heaven eternally. This we ask through Christ Our Lord. Amen.

QUAM OBLATIONEM

~~~~~~

Inasmuch as I become sanctified or oblated in and into Christ, Christ comes to be in me. The Holy Sacrifice *produces* the Holy Sacrament, at Mass and in me, now and forever. We can sense a certain urgency. Christ is coming! Only those whose life-oblation has been blessed into and united with Christ-oblation will lovingly commune with Christ both in time and eternity.

~~~~~~

QUAM OBLATIONEM tu, Deus, in omnibus, quaesumus, bene ✠ dictam, adscrip ✠ tam, ra ✠ tam, rationabilem, acceptabilemque facere digneris: ut nobis Cor ✠ pus, et San ✠ guis fiat dilectissimi Filii tui Domini nostri Jesu Christi.

BLESS ✠ INTO BEING, O Heavenly Father, in and into each of us THE ✠ Oblation. Lead us to know and conform to Thy Revealed ✠ Will so that the Body ✠ and Blood ✠ of Thy adored Son, Our Lord and Saviour, Jesus Christ, may come to dwell in us unto our salvation, now and forever and ever.

THE CONSECRATION

The Canonized Latin words *"Qui pridie quam pateretur..."* by themselves force each priest to rise above ordinary praying-- to start acting and speaking *in persona Christi*, in the *active tense* of Christ-priest.

Thus does the Priest *bless*--by *agens et dicens* – the Divine Transformation into existence *as* Christ decreed on the *pridie,* Good Friday.

As Christ-priest validly *blesses* bread, bread is annihilated. CHRIST – SACRIFICE and SACRAMENT – come into being.

At the Consecration, the Father's eternal Blessing Plan comes to us anew *(benedixit):* through Christ-priest, the Word speaking *(dicens):* the graces and power of the Holy Ghost accomplishing *(gratias agens).*

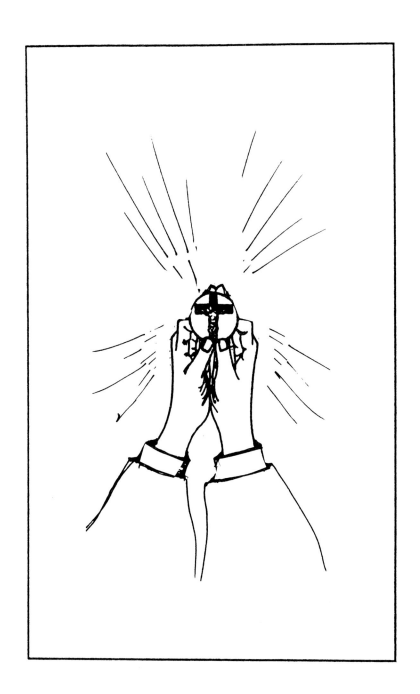

Qui pridie, quam pateretur, accepit panem in sanctas ac venerabiles manus suas, et elevatis oculis in coelum ad te Deum Patrem suum omnipotentem tibi gratias agens, bene ✠ dixit, fregit, deditque discipulis suis, dicens: Accipite, et manducate ex hoc omnes:

HOC EST ENIM CORPUS MEUM.

WHO, at the beginning of (and part of) the Day (Good Friday), on which He suffered THE Oblation into being, HE took bread into His holy and venerable (adored) Hands, having lifted up His eyes towards Heaven to Thee, His Almighty Father, *GRATIAS AGENS*, BLESSED ✠ broke and gave to His disciples SAYING: All of you eat of *HOC*:

for *HOC* is My Body.

~~~~~~

Reflect: **Good Friday comes to us. We are at the Last Supper. We are at Calvary. Christ communes with us. Christ remains with us. Thy Christ-priest brings into his space-time Christ's Saving Deed and thus, Christ, the Saving Person. I am overcome with grateful joy. Because of my sins I am not worthy. MY LORD AND MY GOD!**

~~~~~~

Again, the Canonized Latin words *force* the priest to act and speak *in persona Christi.* Only by properly *agens et dicens,* can he BLESS into being the Mystery of Faith.

~~~~~~

Simili modo postquam coenatum est, accipiens et hunc praeclarum Calicem in sanctas ac venerabiles manus suas: item tibi gratias agens, bene ✠ dixit, deditque discipulis suis, dicens: Accipite, et bibite ex eo omnes:

Hic est enim Calix Sanguinis mei, novi et aeterni testamenti: mysterium fidei: qui pro vobis et pro multis effundetur in remissionem peccatorum.

Replacing the chalice on the corporal, the Priest says:

Haec quotiescumque feceritis, in Mei Memoriam facietis.

Likewise, taking the most precious chalice into His adorable hands, again *GRATIAS AGENS;* He BLESSED ✠ and gave to His disciples SAYING:

"Take and drink from this all of you for THIS is the Chalice of My Blood of the New and Eternal Testament–the Mystery of Faith--Which shall be shed for you and for the many (the multitude of the Elect) unto the forgiveness of sins. As often as you do this, you do INTO THE MEMORY of Me."

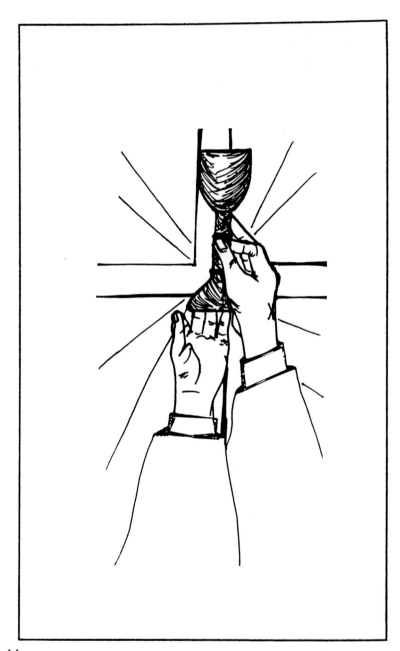

Reflect: Christ's broken Body, my only food, His shed Blood, my only drink, because of Which, we call this Friday Good. I dread such food and drink, lest my body be broken and my blood be shed.

O God, help me to conquer my natural fears by Thy love and graces. Help me to live now, not I, but Christ-crucified in me.

I PRAISE, THANK and ADORE THEE, O Christ, because of Thy Saving-Deed. By Thy Holy Sacrifice, Thou hast redeemed me, a sinner, from eternal Hell.

O JESUS! Each Mass is Calvary realized in an unbloody manner. Each Mass is Heaven realized in a non-glorifying manner. Each Mass is my only forgiveness for sins. How can I escape damnation if I neglect, despise or malign, so great salvation?

Here at Mass the Faith that saves is REALIZED. Here is the Mystery of Faith! Here is Christ's abiding Will and Testament in His Blood! Here is the Sacred Heart of Jesus!

UNDE ET MEMORES

~~~~~~

The totality of the Elect are *born from, part of and within this* Mystery of Faith: *Plebs tua sancta,* all of Thy Holy People, the People of God, the Communion of Saints *actually* and eternally define the Catholic Church–the saints in Heaven now or in the future.

The Sacrifice, *once given* – *DATIS* – and *continually being given* – *DONIS* – is God's Greatest Gift, His (totally effective) Saving Will.

This Saving Will: existed from all eternity, was *embodied* in Christ Jesus, *was* ratified and suffered into being on Good Friday, *is* ratified (*re-done*) at each valid Mass; and, *is* and *will be* ratified eternally so as to constitute or define Heaven (Apoc 5:6-9).

~~~~~~

UNDE ET MEMORES, Domine, nos servi tui, sed et plebs tua sancta, ejusdem Christi Filii tui, Domini nostri tam beatae Passionis, nec non et ab inferis Resurrectionis, sed et in coelos gloriosae Ascensionis: offerimus praeclarae majestati tuae de tuis donis ac datis, hostiam ✠ puram, hostiam ✠ sanctam, hostiam ✠ immaculatam, Panem ✠ sanctum vitae aeternae, et Calicem ✠ salutis perpetuae.

THUS, *(unde)* through the mystery of faith done into *the* Memory, are we, Thy abject slaves, Thy Holy People, saved from Hell and made into *memores* of the same Jesus Christ Our Lord, Thy Son. We, Thy Holy People, are taken into Christ's Passion, into His Resurrection from the realm of death; and into His glorious Ascension into Heaven. We offer to Thy Divine Majesty (of, from and because of) *the once given* and *the continually being given*:

THE PURE ✠ VICTIM; THE SANCTIFYING ✠ VICTIM; THE SIN-CONQUERING ✠ VICTIM-- the Holy ✠ Bread:

the Source, Sustenance and Summit of eternal life and the Chalice ✠ of our perpetually being saved from Hell and unto Heaven.

SUPRA QUAE

~~~~~~

Mass prayers focus on *your* oblation in and into Christ and His Oblation. May Mass avail unto *your* salvation.

~~~~~~

SUPRA QUAE propitio ac sereno vultu respicere digneris: et accepta habere, sicuti accepta habere dignatus es munera pueri tui justi Abel, et sacrificium patriarchae nostri Abrahae: et quod tibi obtulit summus sacerdos tuus Melchisedech, sanctum sacrificium, immaculatam hostiam.

Deign to look upon our oblations with a favorable and gracious countenance, and to accept our oblations as Thou didst accept the oblation of Thy just servant Abel, and the sacrifice of our patriarch Abraham, and that which Thy high priest Melchisedech offered up to Thee, the Holy Sacrifice, the Immaculate Victim.

SUPPLICES

SUPPLICES te rogamus, omnipotens Deus: jube haec perferri per manus sancti Angeli tui in sublime altare tuum, in conspectu divinae majestatis tuae: ut quotquot (he kisses the altar) *ex hac altaris participatione, sacrosanctum Filii tui Cor ✠ pus et San ✠ guinem sumpserimus, omni benedictione coelesti et gratia repleamur. Per eumdem Christum Dominum nostrum. Amen.*

With greatest humility, fear and reverence, we beg Thee, Almighty God, that *HAEC OBLATIONES* -- the offerings or oblations of us ordinary people, Thy *quotquot* (people) striving to be full and authentic oblations through and in Christ – may somehow be taken before Thy Divine Majesty, to Thy Holy Altar above so that we *quotquot* who dare to receive the Body ✠ and Blood ✠ of Christ may be filled with graces and blessings from Heaven, through the same Christ our Lord. Amen.

MEMENTO

MEMENTO etiam, Domine, famulorum famularumque tuarum N... et N..., qui nos praecesserunt cum signo fidei, et dormiunt in somno pacis. Ipsis, Domine, et omnibus in Christo quiescentibus, locum refrigerii, lucis et pacis, ut indulgeas, deprecamur. Per eumdem Christum Dominum nostrum. Amen.

MEMENTO, make into Thy Memory, O Lord, Thy servants and handmaids, N... and N..., who have gone before us with the sign of faith, and rest in the sleep of peace. To these, O Lord, and to all who rest in Christ, we beseech Thee to grant of Thy goodness, the place of comfort, light and peace. Through the same Christ our Lord. Amen.

NOBIS QUOQUE

~~~~~~

Pray this prayer with great conviction and sincerity. *You are a sinner--a sinner by birth and inclination, a sinner in deed and in habit.* As the Priest strikes his chest, humbly join him acknowledging that you, too, are a *sinner.*

~~~~~~

Nobis quoque peccatoribus famulis tuis, de multitudine miserationum tuarum sperantibus, partem aliquam et societatem donare digneris, cum tuis sanctis Apostolis et Martyribus: cum Joanne, Stephano, Matthia, Barnaba, Ignatio, Alexandro, Marcellino, Petro, Felicitate, Perpetua, Agatha, Lucia, Agnete, Caecilia, Anastasia, et omnibus Sanctis tuis: intra quorum nos consortium, non aestimator meriti, sed veniae, quaesumus, largitor admitte. Per Christum Dominum nostrum.

To us *sinners*, grant, O Lord, a place with Thy holy Apostles, martyrs, and all other saints. Look not upon our *merits*, or upon what we deserve, but in Thy great Mercy, pardon us our *sins*, through Jesus Christ, Our Lord.

PER CHRISTUM

Christ is *the Priest* or *Pontifex* for the Elect. Through Him they go to God and through Him, God comes to them. All that is good for the Elect comes from Christ. All that is for God's positive external glory from His Elect comes through, with and in *CHRIST.*

Per quem haec omnia, Domine, semper bona creas, sancti ✠ ficas, vivi ✠ ficas, bene ✠ dicis, et praestas nobis.

Through Christ Our Lord, do Thou, Heavenly Father and Holy Ghost, create ✠ and provide; transform ✠ and sanctify ✠ Thine Elect and that which Thou dost graciously bestow upon them.

Uncovering the chalice, the Priest genuflects and makes the Sign of the Cross with the Sacred Host five times:

Per ip ✠ sum, et cum ip ✠ so, et in ip ✠ so, est tibi Deo Patri ✠ omnipotenti, in unitate Spiritus ✠ Sancti, omnis honor et gloria. Per omnia saecula saeculorum.
S. Amen.

Through ✠ Him, with ✠ Him and in ✠ Him is to Thee, God, the Father ✠ Almighty, in unity with the Holy ✠ Ghost all honor and glory, world without end.
S. Amen.

PATER NOSTER

Oremus. Praeceptis salutaribus moniti, et divina institutione formati, audemus dicere:

PATER NOSTER, qui es in coelis: sanctificetur nomen tuum: adveniat regnum tuum: fiat voluntas tua, sicut in coelo, et in terra. Panem nostrum quotidianum da nobis hodie: Et dimitte nobis debita nostra, sicut et nos dimittimus debitoribus nostris. Et ne nos inducas in tentationem.

Having been commanded by Thee to pray thus in order to be saved from Hell, we dare to boldly proclaim these precious words--words given to us by Thee, Jesus Christ, Our Lord and Saviour.

OUR FATHER, Who art in heaven, hallowed be Thy Name; Thy Kingdom come; Thy Will be done on earth as it is in heaven. Give us this day our daily bread; and forgive us our trespasses, as we forgive those who trespass against us. And lead us not into temptation.

S. Sed libera nos a malo.
But deliver us from evil.

P. Amen.

LIBERA NOS

Taking the paten, the Priest prays:

LIBERA NOS, quaesumus, Domine, ab omnibus malis, praeteritis, praesentibus, et futuris: et intercedente beata et gloriosa semper Virgine Dei Genitrice Maria, cum beatis Apostolis tuis Petro et Paulo, atque Andrea, et omnibus Sanctis, ✠ (making the Sign of the Cross on himself) *da propitius pacem in diebus nostris: ut ope misericordiae tuae adjuti, et a peccato simus semper liberi, et ab omni perturbatione securi.*

DELIVER US, we beseech Thee, O Lord, from all evils, past, present and to come, and by the intercession of the Blessed and glorious ever Virgin Mary, Mother of God, together with Thy blessed Apostles Peter and Paul, and Andrew, and all the Saints, ✠ mercifully grant peace in our days, that through Thy loving Mercy, we may be always free from sin and its effects. Sanctify us. Purge us from sin. Make us worthy to commune with Christ, now and forever.

FRACTIO ET COMMIXTIO

Concluding the *Libera Nos,* Christ-priest genuflects and breaks *HOC*–the Sacred Host– into two, placing Half on the paten, breaking off a Particle from the Other saying:

Per eumdem Dominum nostrum Jesum Christum Filium tuum. Qui tecum vivit et regnat in unitate Spiritus Sancti Deus. Per omnia saecula saeculorum.
Through the same Jesus Christ Thy Son, Our Lord Who lives and reigns with Thee in the unity of the Holy Ghost, God. World without end.
S. Amen.

Christ-priest makes the Sign of the Cross with the Particle over the Chalice saying:

P. Pax ✠ Domini sit ✠ semper vobis ✠ cum.
May the peace ✠ of the Lord ✠ be always with ✠ you.

S. Et cum spiritu tuo.
And with thy spirit.

Christ-priest drops the Particle into the Chalice, saying:

Haec commixtio et consecratio Corporis et Sanguinis Domini nostri Jesu Christi fiat accipientibus nobis in vitam aeternam. Amen.
May the Body and Blood of Our Lord Jesus Christ bring those of us who receive Holy Communion unto eternal life in Heaven. Amen.

~~~~~~

In a mystical/sacramental way, the Consecration separates Christ's broken Body from His shed Blood. Now the breaking of HOC and the uniting of the Sacred Species "physically signs" Christ-glorified, Holy Sacrament.

"What" was effected by separate consecrations (Holy Sacrifice) is now mystically fulfilled as "union of Sacred Species," in Christ-Glorified, "Holy Sacrament." Now the Mass prayers focus on Christ-Glorified, Holy Eucharist.

~~~~~~

DAY OF WRATH, that inevitable day of God's Judgment...who for me will be interceding when decent people will be in dire need of mercy?

O Good Jesus! Please remember that I am the reason for Thy coming to be. Be then my Saviour. O Lamb Once Slain, Who for all eternity, will be the Adored Source, Sustenance and Summit of Heaven for the Elect:

O Lamb of God Who takest away sins, grant me the peace of eternal Heaven. Lamb of God, have mercy on me!

AGNUS DEI

AGNUS DEI, qui tollis peccata mundi: miserere nobis.
LAMB OF GOD, Who takest away the sins of the world, have mercy on us.
Agnus Dei, qui tollis peccata mundi: miserere nobis.
Lamb of God, Who takest away the sins of the world, have mercy on us.
Agnus Dei, qui tollis peccata mundi: dona nobis pacem.
Lamb of God, Who takest away the sins of the world, grant us peace.

THE PRIEST'S PREPARATION FOR COMMUNION

~~~~~~

These prayers remind the Priest Whom he is to receive in Holy Communion. Christ is the God-man. He is the Second Person of the Triune God. He alone is Saviour.

~~~~~~

Domine, Jesu Christe, qui dixisti Apostolis tuis: Pacem relinquo vobis, pacem meam do vobis: ne respicias peccata mea, sed fidem Ecclesiae tuae: eamque secundum voluntatem tuam pacificare et coadunare digneris: Qui vivis et regnas Deus per omnia saecula saeculorum. Amen.

O Lord, Jesus Christ, Who didst say to Thine Apostles: Peace I leave you, My peace I give you: look not upon my sins, but upon the faith of Thy existential Church: and deign to give her that peace and unity which is agreeable to Thy will: God Who livest and reignest world without end. Amen.

Domine Jesu Christe, Fili Dei vivi, qui ex voluntate Patris, cooperante Spiritu Sancto, per mortem tuam mundum vivificasti: libera me per hoc sacrosanctum Corpus et Sanguinem tuum ab omnibus iniquitatibus meis, et universis malis: et fac me tuis semper inhaerere mandatis, et a te numquam separari permittas. Qui cum eodem Deo Patre, et Spiritu Sancto vivis et regnas Deus in saecula saeculorum. Amen.

O Lord Jesus Christ, Son of the living God, Who, by the will of the Father and the co-operation of the Holy Ghost, hast by Thy death given life to the world: deliver me by this, Thy most sacred Body and Blood, from all my iniquities and from every evil: make me cling always to Thy commandments, and never permit me to be separated from Thee. Who with the Father and the Holy Ghost, livest and reignest God, world without end. Amen.

Perceptio Corporis tui, Domine Jesu Christe, quod ego indignus sumere praesumo, non mihi proveniat in judicium et condemnationem: sed pro tua pietate prosit mihi ad tutamentum mentis et corporis, et ad medelam percipiendam. Qui vivis et regnas cum Deo Patre in unitate Spiritus Sancti Deus, per omnia saecula saeculorum. Amen.

Let not the partaking of Thy Body, O Lord Jesus Christ, which I, though unworthy, presume to receive, turn to my judgment and condemnation; but through Thy mercy may it be unto me a safeguard and a healing remedy both of soul and body. Who livest and reignest with God the Father in the unity of the Holy Ghost, God, world without end. Amen.

COMMUNION OF THE PRIEST

The Priest genuflects and then says:

Panem coelestem accipiam, et nomen Domini invocabo.
I will take the Bread of Heaven and will call upon the Name of the Lord.

Striking his breast, and saying the opening words audibly, he says three times:

DOMINE, NON SUM DIGNUS, ut intres sub tectum meum: sed tantum dic verbo, et sanabitur anima mea.

LORD, I AM NOT WORTHY that Thou shouldst enter under my roof; but only say the word, and my soul will be healed.

Making the Sign of the Cross with *HOC*–Sacred Host–over the paten, Christ-priest prays,

Corpus ✠ *Domini nostri Jesu Christi custodiat animam meam in vitam aeternam. Amen.*
May the Body ✠ of Our Lord Jesus Christ preserve my soul unto life everlasting . Amen.

He then reverently receives both Halves of the Sacred Host. He uncovers the chalice, genuflects, collects whatever *Fragments* may remain on the corporal, and purifies the paten over the chalice, saying,

Quid retribuam Domino pro omnibus quae retribuit mihi? Calicem salutaris accipiam, et nomen Domini invocabo. Laudans invocabo Dominum, et ab inimicis meis salvus ero.
What return shall I make to the Lord for all the things that He hath given unto me? I will take the chalice of salvation, and call upon the Name of the Lord. I will call upon the Lord and praise Him in order to be saved from my enemies.

Making the Sign of the Cross with the chalice, he says,

Sanguis ✠ *Domini nostri Jesu Christi custodiat animam meam in vitam aeternam. Amen.*
May the Blood ✠ of Our Lord Jesus Christ preserve my soul unto life everlasting. Amen.

Christ-priest then reverently consumes the Precious Blood.

~~~~~~

Signs of the Cross over Christ remind *us*– especially, the celebrant of Mass–that Christ must now be perceived as Christ-crucified. These *crosses over Christ* obviously are *not* the Priest's blessings of Christ.

~~~~~~

COMMUNION OF THE FAITHFUL

Turning toward the people, the Priest says,

Misereatur vestri omnipotens Deus, et dimissis peccatis vestris, perducat vos ad vitam aeternam. Amen.

May Almighty God have mercy on you, forgive you your sins, and bring you to life everlasting. Amen.

Indulgentiam, ✠ *absolutionem, et remissionem peccatorum vestrorum tribuat vobis omnipotens, et misericors Dominus. S. Amen.*
May the Almighty and Merciful Lord grant you pardon, absolution and remission of your sins. Amen.

Turning toward the people, Christ-priest elevates the Sacred Host saying:

ECCE AGNUS DEI, ecce qui tollit peccata mundi.
BEHOLD, THE LAMB OF GOD, behold Him Who taketh away the sins of the world.

DOMINE, NON SUM DIGNUS, ut intres sub tectum meum: sed tantum dic verbo, et sanabitur anima mea.
LORD, I AM NOT WORTHY that Thou should enter under my roof, say but the word and my soul will be healed. (Repeat three times.)

As Christ-priest goes to the Altar rail and gives Holy Communion, he also gives a personal benediction by signing with the Holy Eucharist, saying to each person:

Corpus ✠ *Domini nostri Jesu Christi custodiat animam tuam in vitam aeternam. Amen.*
May the Body ✠ of Our Lord Jesus Christ preserve your soul unto life everlasting. Amen.

HOLY COMMUNION

PRAYERS

With Communion, Jesus enters my heart and remains corporally present in me as long as the species (the appearance) of bread lasts; that is, for about 15 minutes. During this time, the Holy Fathers teach that the angels surround me to continue to adore Jesus and love Him without interruption.

> **"When Jesus is corporally present within you, the angels surround you as a guard of love."**
> **St. Bernard**

> **"If the angels could envy, they would envy us for Holy Communion."**
> **Pope Saint Pius X**

SUSCIPE OF ST. IGNATIUS LOYOLA

TAKE, O LORD, and receive my entire liberty, my memory, my understanding, and my whole will.

ALL THAT I AM AND ALL THAT I POSSESS, Thou hast given me: I surrender it all to Thee to be disposed of according to Thy Will.

GIVE ME ONLY THY LOVE AND THY GRACE; with these I will be rich enough, and I desire nothing more.

ANIMA CHRISTI

SOUL OF CHRIST, sanctify me. BODY OF CHRIST, save me. BLOOD OF CHRIST, give me life. WATER from the side of Christ, wash me. PASSION OF CHRIST, strengthen me.

O GOOD JESUS, hear me. WITHIN THY WOUNDS, hide me. NEVER PERMIT me to be separated from Thee. FROM THE MALIGNANT ENEMY, defend me, AT THE HOUR OF DEATH, call me, and bid me come to Thee, that with Thy saints I may praise Thee forever and ever. Amen.

I FIRMLY BELIEVE

MY GOD, I firmly believe that Thou art bodily present in the Blessed Sacrament of the Altar. I adore Thee here present, from the depths of my heart, and I worship Thy presence with all possible humility. Lord, I thank Thee for allowing me to receive Thee in Holy Communion.

WHAT JOY for my soul to have Jesus Christ always present with us, and to be able to speak to Him, heart to heart with all confidence. Lord, I thank Thee for tabernacling among us.

O LORD, grant that after having adored Thy Divine Majesty here on earth in this wonderful Sacrament, I may be able to adore Thee eternally in Heaven. Amen.

GENTLE JESUS

GENTLE JESUS, Shepherd tender, BREAD OF LIFE to me doth render. SAVE MY SOUL by grace and feeding. HELP ME FOLLOW in Thy leading. GUIDE ME to Thy Life above.

PRIEST'S ABLUTIONS

Wine is poured into the chalice. The Priest drinks it and recalling our reception of Holy Communion, says:

Quod ore sumpsimus, Domine, pura mente capiamus: et de munere temporali fiat nobis remedium sempiternum.
Grant, O Lord, that what we have received with our mouth, we may assimilate with pure minds; and that this temporal gift may become for us an everlasting remedy and the eternal Source of Beatific Life.

Wine and water are poured into the chalice over the fingers of the Priest, who dries them with the purificator, saying silently:

Corpus tuum, Domine, quod sumpsi, et Sanguis quem potavi, adhaereat visceribus meis: et praesta; ut in me non remaneat scelerum macula, quem pura et sancta refecerunt sacramenta: Qui vivis et regnas in saecula saeculorum. Amen.
May the sacramental reception of Thy Body, O Lord, which I have eaten and Thy Blood which I have drunk, become part of my innermost being, and grant that no stain of sin remain in me. May this pure and holy Sacrament transform me, O God, Who livest and reignest forever. Amen.

Christ-priest drinks the wine and water, and the chalice is purified and veiled. He goes to the Epistle side and reads the **COMMUNION VERSE** from the Missal.

COMMUNION VERSE

●*COMMUNION*--PROPER--Today's Mass ●

Following the **COMMUNION VERSE PROPER** to this Mass the Priest turns to the people and says:

P. *Dominus vobiscum.* **The Lord be with you.**
S. *Et cum spiritu tuo.* **And with thy spirit. Amen.**
OREMUS. **Let us pray.**

●*POSTCOMMUNION*--PROPER--Today's Mass●

The Priest prays the **POSTCOMMUNION** prayer from the **PROPER** of the Mass. If the GLORIA was omitted, the Priest omits the *Ite, Missa est* and says instead, *Benedicamus Domino:* Let us bless the Lord, or in Requiem Masses: the priest omits the *Ite, Missa est,* and says aloud: *Requiescant in pace. S. Amen.*

The Priest turns to the people and says:

72

P. *Dominus vobiscum.* **The Lord be with you.**
S. *Et cum spiritu tuo.* **And with thy spirit.**
P. *Ite, Missa est.* **Go, the Mass is ended.**
S. *Deo gratias.* **Thanks be to God.**

~~~~~~

The Sacrifice of the Mass has come to an end. *Ite, Missa est*--from this, the Mass derives its name. The Priest has sent (*missa*) prayers up to God. Christ is the Victim sent (*missa*) to us. And the Victim has been sent (*missa est*) TO GOD on our behalf, as St. Thomas states (Summa theol., q.83, a.4, ad 9).

~~~~~~

Placeat tibi, sancta Trinitas, obsequium servitutis meae: et praesta: ut sacrificium, quod oculis tuae majestatis indignus obtuli, tibi sit acceptabile, mihique, et omnibus, pro quibus illud obtuli, sit te miserante propitiabile. Per Christum Dominum nostrum. Amen.

May the tribute of my homage be pleasing to Thee, O most Holy Trinity. Grant that the Sacrifice which I, unworthy as I am, have offered in the presence of Thy Majesty, may be acceptable to Thee. Through Thy mercy may it be *effective* **unto the forgiveness of my sins and of the sins of those for whom I have offered it. Through Christ our Lord. Amen.**

You have been baptized.
You have been given many
graces. *Now* make all of
these signs of your *election*
sure or *more firm (2 Pe
1:10)*. He Who has begun
this good work in you surely
wants to complete it (Phil
1:6).

Ask God for His graces.
Without Him you can do
nothing. Trust Him. Love
Him. Surrender to His Will.
Agonize to be oblated
through, with and in Christ.
There is no shortcut to
Heaven!

✠

THE BLESSING

The Priest makes the Sign of the Cross over the congregation:

BENEDICAT vos omnipotens Deus: Pater, et Filius, ✠ et Spiritus Sanctus.
May the Almighty God bless you: the Father and the Son ✠ and the Holy Ghost.
S. Amen.

P. Dominus vobiscum. **The Lord be with you.**
S. Et cum spiritu tuo. **And with thy spirit.**

INITIUM SANCTI EVANGELII SECUNDUM JOANNEM

Making the Sign of the Cross first upon the Altar, then upon his forehead, lips and breast, the Priest begins the Gospel ✠ according to St. John:

P. Initium ✠ sancti Evangelii secundum Joannem.
S. Gloria tibi, Domine. **Glory be to Thee, O Lord.**

IN PRINCIPIO erat Verbum, et Verbum erat apud Deum, et Deus erat Verbum. Hoc erat in principio apud Deum. Omnia per ipsum facta sunt: et sine ipso factum est nihil quod factum est: in ipso vita erat, et vita erat lux hominum: et lux in tenebris lucet, et tenebrae eam non comprehenderunt.

Fuit homo missus a Deo, cui nomen erat Joannes. Hic venit in testimonium, ut testimonium perhiberet de lumine, ut omnes crederent per illum. Non erat ille lux, sed ut testimonium perhiberet de lumine.

Erat lux vera, quae illuminat omnem hominem venientem in hunc mundum. In mundo erat, et mundus per ipsum factus est, et mundus eum non cognovit. In propria venit, et sui eum non receperunt. Quotquot autem receperunt eum, dedit eis potestatem filios Dei fieri, his, qui credunt in nomine ejus: qui non ex sanguinibus, neque ex voluntate carnis, neque ex voluntate viri, sed ex Deo nati sunt. *(Hic genuflectur)*

ET VERBUM CARO FACTUM EST, et habitavit in nobis: et vidimus gloriam ejus, gloriam quasi Unigeniti a Patre, plenum gratiae et veritatis.

S. Deo gratias.

THE BEGINNING OF THE HOLY GOSPEL ACCORDING TO ST. JOHN

IN THE BEGINNING was the Word, and the Word was with God; and the Word was God. He was in the beginning with God. All things were made through Him, and without Him was made nothing that has been made. In Him was life, and the life was the light of men. And the light shines in the darkness; and the darkness grasped it not. There was a man, sent from God, whose name was John. This man came as a witness, to give testimony of the Light, that all might believe through Him. He was not himself the Light, but was to bear witness to the Light. It was the true Light that enlightens every man who comes into the world. He was in the world, and the world was made by Him, but the world knew Him not. He came unto His own, and His own received Him not. But to as many as received Him, *quotquot,* He gave the power of becoming sons of God; to those who believe in His name: who were born not of blood, nor of the will of the flesh, nor of the will of man, but of God. (Genuflect)

And the WORD WAS MADE FLESH and dwelt among us. And we saw His glory, the glory as of the Only-begotten of the Father, full of grace and truth.

S. Thanks be to God.

78

PRAYERS AFTER MASS

Usually, the Leonine prayers are said after Mass. We pray for the conversion of Russia and for our freedom from the temporal and eternal effects of Russia's Errors-- the enthronement of *man* and the dethronement of God *as revealed.*

AVE MARIA-THE HAIL MARY

AVE, MARIA, gratia plena; Dominus tecum: benedicta tu in mulieribus, et benedictus fructus ventris tui Jesus.

SANCTA MARIA, Mater Dei, ora pro nobis peccatoribus, nunc et in hora mortis nostrae. Amen.

HAIL, MARY, full of grace. The Lord is with thee. Blessed art thou among women and blessed is the fruit of thy womb, Jesus.

HOLY MARY, Mother of God, pray for us sinners, now and at the hour of our death. Amen. (3 times)

SALVE REGINA--HAIL HOLY QUEEN

SALVE, REGINA, Mater misericoridiae, vita, dulcedo, et spes nostra, salve. Ad te clamamus exsules filii Evae. Ad te suspiramus gementes et flentes in hac lacrymarum valle. Eia ergo, advocata nostra, illos tuos misericordes oculos ad nos converte. Et Jesum benedictum fructum ventris tui, nobis, post hoc exilium ostende.

O clemens, O pia, O dulcis Virgo Maria.

HAIL, HOLY QUEEN, Mother of Mercy, our life, our sweetness and our hope! To thee do we cry, poor banished children of Eve; to thee do we send up our sighs, mourning and weeping in this valley of tears. Turn then, most gracious advocate, thine eyes of mercy towards us; and after this our exile, show unto us the blessed fruit of thy womb, Jesus.

O clement, O loving, O sweet Virgin Mary.

P. Ora pro nobis, sancta Dei Genitrix.
Pray for us, O holy Mother of God.

S. Ut digni efficiamur promissionibus Christi.
That we may be made worthy of the promises of Christ.

Oremus. **Let us pray.**

DEUS, refugium nostrum et virtus, populum ad te clamantem propitius respice, et intercedente gloriosa et Immaculata Virgine Dei Genitrice Maria, cum beato Joseph ejus Sponso, ac beatis Apostolis tuis Petro et Paulo, et omnibus Sanctis, quas pro conversione peccatorum, pro libertate et exaltatione sanctae Matris Ecclesiae preces effundimus, misericors et benignus exaudi. Per eumdem Christum Dominum nostrum.

S. Amen.

O GOD, our refuge, and our strength, look down in mercy on Thy people who cry to Thee; and by the intercession of the glorious and Immaculate Virgin Mary, Mother of God, of Saint Joseph her spouse, of Thy blessed Apostles Peter and Paul, and of all the Saints, in mercy and goodness, hear our prayers for the conversion of sinners, and for the liberty and exaltation of our holy mother, the Church, through the same Christ our Lord.

Amen.

PRAYER TO ST. MICHAEL

SANCTE MICHAEL, Archangele, defende nos in proelio; contra nequitiam et insidias diaboli esto praesidium.

Imperet illi Deus; supplices deprecamur: tuque, Princeps militiae coelestis, Satanam aliosque spiritus malignos, qui ad perditionem animarum pervagantur in mundo, divina virtute in infernum detrude.

S. Amen.

ST. MICHAEL, the Archangel, defend us in battle; be our safeguard against the wickedness and snares of the devil.

May God rebuke him we humbly pray; and do Thou, Prince of the heavenly host, by the power of God, cast into Hell Satan and all the evil spirits, who wander through the world seeking the ruin of souls.

Amen.

P. Cor Jesu sacratissimum.
Most Sacred Heart of Jesus.

S. Miserere nobis. (3 times)
Have mercy on us. (3 times)

PATER NOSTER-OUR FATHER
An Exegesis

PATER NOSTER, qui es in coelis: sanctificetur nomen tuum: adveniat regnum tuum: fiat voluntas tua, sicut in coelo, et in terra. Panem nostrum quotidianum da nobis hodie: Et dimitte nobis debita nostra, sicut et nos dimittimus debitoribus nostris. Et ne nos inducas in tentationem. Sed libera nos a malo.
Amen.

OUR FATHER, Who art in heaven, hallowed be Thy Name (be Thou fittingly praised and adored); **Thy Kingdom come** (Thy Divine Liturgy of Heaven come to earth); **Thy Will be done on earth** (Thy Salutary Will, by which sinners are saved from Hell through Thy unbloody Holy Sacrifice of the Canonized Mass) **as it is in Heaven** (the "worship of the Lamb that was slain").

Give us this day our daily bread (Holy Sacrament from Holy Sacrifice of the Divine Liturgy)**; and forgive us our trespasses, as we forgive those who trespass against us** (forgive our injustices to Thee as we forgive "injustice" to us). **And lead us not into temptation** (the temptation to "'do' man's liturgy" in place of God's Divine Liturgy). **But deliver us from evil** (the evil of man's liturgy–which has no salutary value). **Amen.**

FINAL REFLECTIONS

LORD JESUS, ever grace me to pray and to live the Holy Sacrifice--Christ-Crucified--every moment of my life. Only inasmuch as I do so, do I participate in the Mass. Only if I do so on earth, will I live united to Christ eternally in Heaven.

BY THY HOLY GHOST, inspire and empower me to be *Christ-Oblated*--to do all into Thy Memory. Grace me to pray and to live the Mass as Thou desire--into *Thy Memory*, being Christ-Oblated, being conformed to Christ-Crucified.

MAY I COME TO LIVE, not me, but Christ-Oblated, Christ-Crucified in me. May I come to pray and live the Mass ever more fully every moment of my life.

WHENEVER THOU, O Lord Jesus, livest in anyone this side of death, Thou livest to die. I pray that in every moment within and between my Holy Communions that Thou dost inspire and *actualize* me to live, not me, but Thou in me--Christ-Crucified, Christ, obedient to God the Father, unto death. Only *thus* can I be saved from Hell.

ACCORDING TO THY WILL, salvation comes through Mary. I also realize Thy Mother is given to me to help me to conform to Thee, so that I will be her child--not Eve's--now and forever.

LEAD ME, O LORD, to devoutly pray the Rosary Thou hast given us through the Blessed Virgin Mary.

HELP ME TO PRAY these Rosary Mysteries recalling that all of the mysteries of Salvation save the Elect from Hell. The Salutary Mysteries constitute *THE MEMORY*, Christ-Oblated, Christ-Crucified-- *the* Mystery of Faith, the Mass itself.

All OF THE SALUTARY MYSTERIES are made present and adored at the Holy Sacrifice–now and eternally. It is my great privilege to pray the Rosary. May each Rosary recall the last Mass I attended and prepare me for the next Mass as well as for the Eternal Mass of Heaven.

I THANK THEE, LORD JESUS, for the Rosary. The Rosary helps me to pray the Mass, *the Lamb Once Slain,* the only source of true Life.

In this horrible sin-immersed world in which I now live, Lord Jesus, ever prevent me from joining the sinfully proud. Help me to live humbly confessing that I am a sinner, one of the *gestating quotquot (Jn*

1). By Thy grace, I confess that Thy Saving Will, Thy Saving Deed and Thy Saving Person constitute my *only* need, my *only* hope and my *only* way of avoiding eternal Hell.

MY ONLY SAVIOUR, forgive my sins and save me from the fires of Hell. Make me, O Lord, in Thy Loving-Mercy, a beneficiary of Thy New and Eternal Testament brought into being by Thy Holy Sacrifice.

HELP ME TO DISCERN in order to attend the valid (by Thy grace) Holy Sacrifice of the Mass in order to participate unto my salvation from Hell. May I always thirst for Masses--as a thirst-driven deer seeks the stream of clean, living water.

May I go from each valid Mass, the *only* stream of Life, eucharistically--*gratias agens--doing* or living out the graces attained at the Masses I have attended. May I come to pray and live the Mass, the Holy Sacrifice, in grateful adoration of Thy Sacred Loving and Merciful Heart and, in grateful thanksgiving and love for the perfect God-loving Heart of Thy Mother, Whom Thou hast given to me at the Holy Sacrifice to be my mother as well. Amen.